CB128312

NATURAL SCIENCE
PRIMARY 1

BY ME

ACTIVITY BOOK

UNIT 1 All about me

1 Say and trace. Match.

arm

tummy

leg

hand

foot

2 Colour. Find the words.

head

torso

limbs

n	t	m	e	h	l	r
w	h	e	a	d	i	n
s	a	b	g	y	m	f
o	i	f	l	k	b	h
a	p	t	o	r	s	o

3 Look and circle.

neck | wrist

elbow | ankle

shoulder | knee

ankle | hip

4 Read and draw. Write.

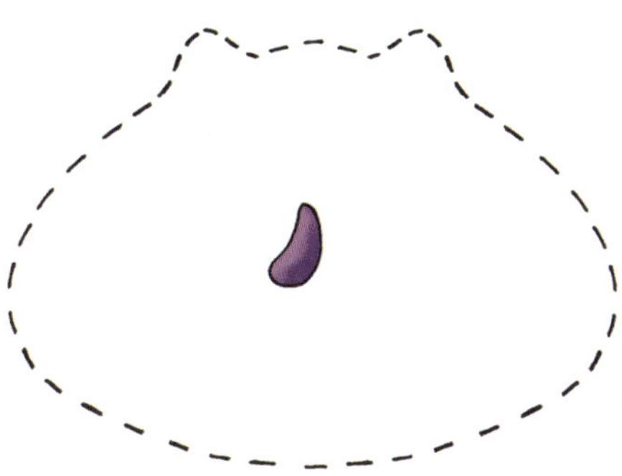

I have 3 red legs,
5 green eyes,
4 orange arms,
a big blue mouth and
a little purple nose.

What colour is your monster's body?

5 Trace and match.

I feel happy

I feel angry

I feel worried

6 Who is being kind? Put a tick (✓) or a cross (✗).

7 Write.

touch taste see ~~hear~~

hear

8 Draw.

my favourite taste

my favourite smell

Let's investigate at home!

Make a puppet that moves

1

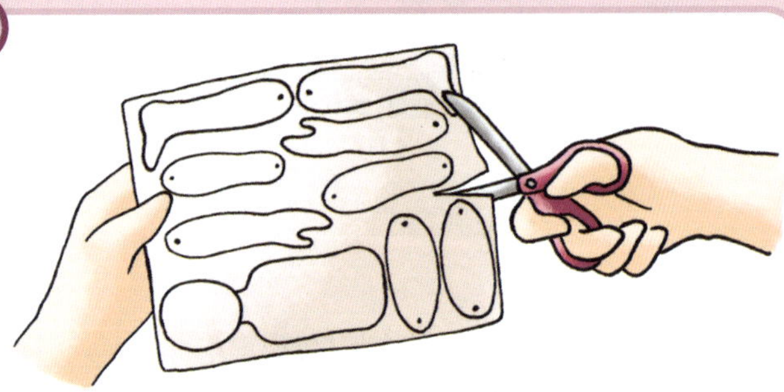

Cut out the body parts.

2

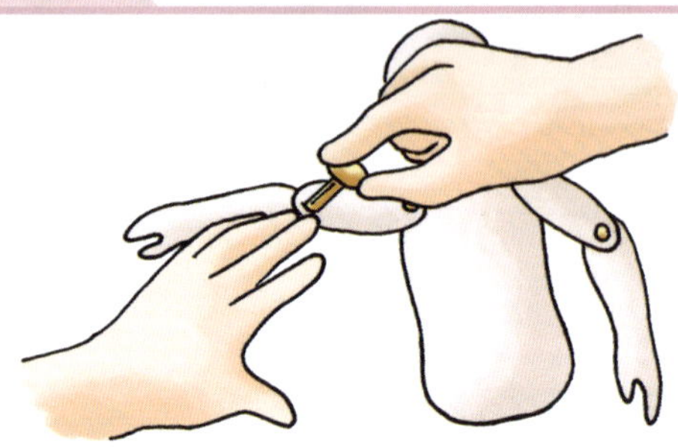

Connect the shoulders and elbows.

3

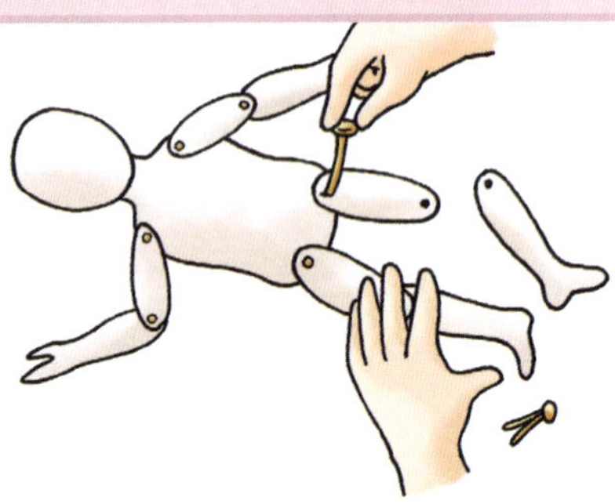

Connect the hips and knees.

4

Colour. Move your puppet.

1 Write *yes* or *no*.

Can your puppet bend its knees? ______

Can your puppet wave? ______

Skills check

1 Look and read. Put a tick (✓) or a cross (✗).
Look at the two examples.

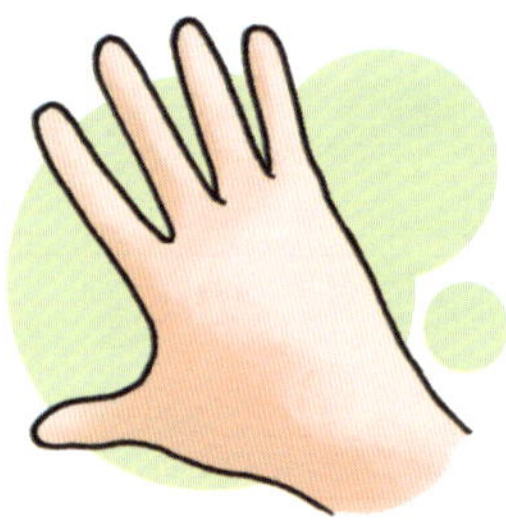

This is a hand. ✓

This is an ear. ✗

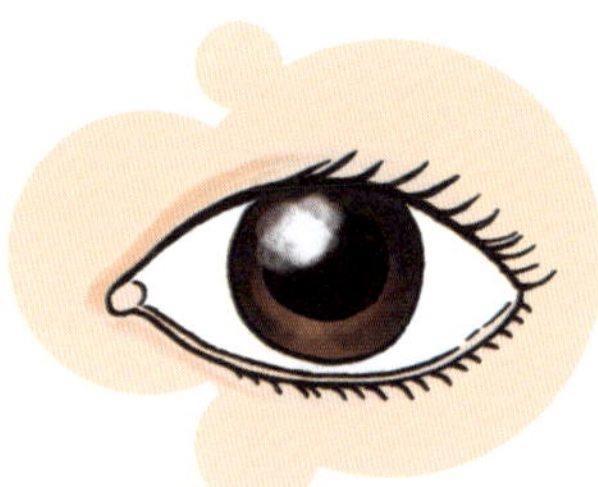

1 This is an eye. ☐

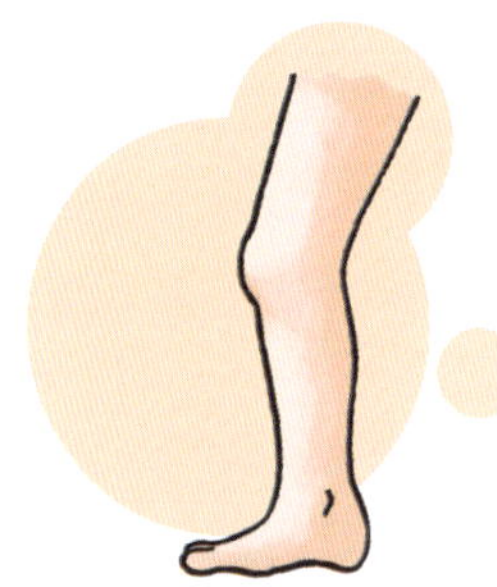

2 This is a leg. ☐

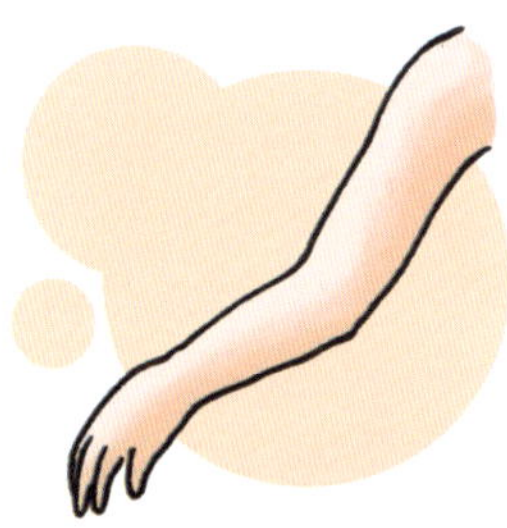

3 This is a foot. ☐

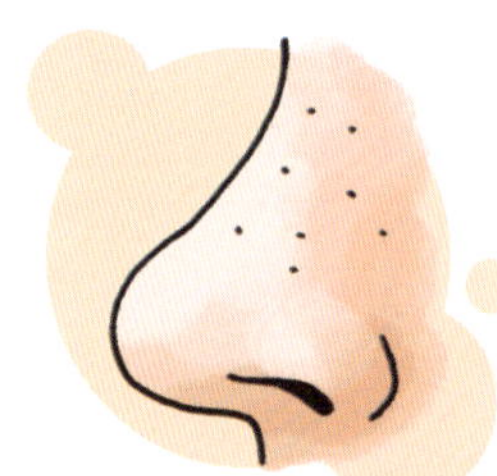

4 This is a nose. ☐

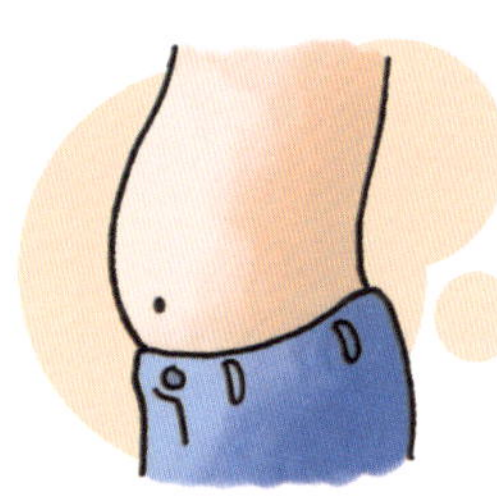

5 This is a mouth. ☐

UNIT 2

Healthy habits

1 Put the food in the correct group. Draw lines.

2 Draw your favourite food from the food group.

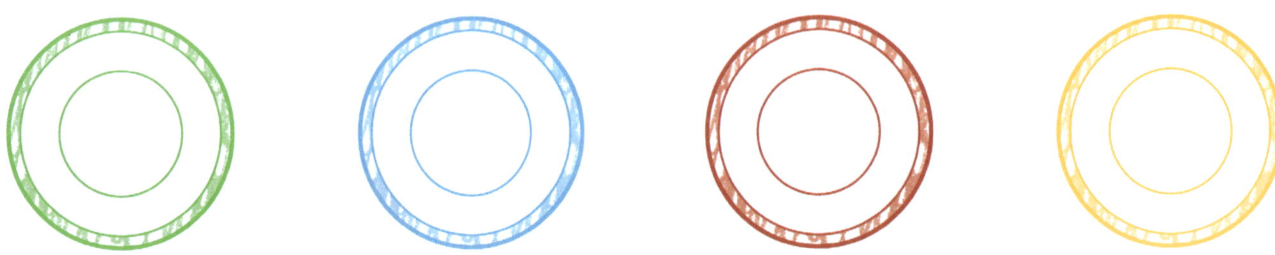

3 Write (F) fruit or (V) vegetable.

F  apple

 lettuce

 banana

 beans

 carrot

 strawberry

4 Food comes from plants and animals. Match.

5 Match.

6 Trace. Circle the healthy meals.

breakfast | lunch | dinner

7 Put the snacks in the correct group.

yoghurt 

grapes 

lollipop 

chocolate 

cereal bar 

crisps 

healthy snacks	unhealthy snacks
yoghurt	

8 Read and circle the correct word.

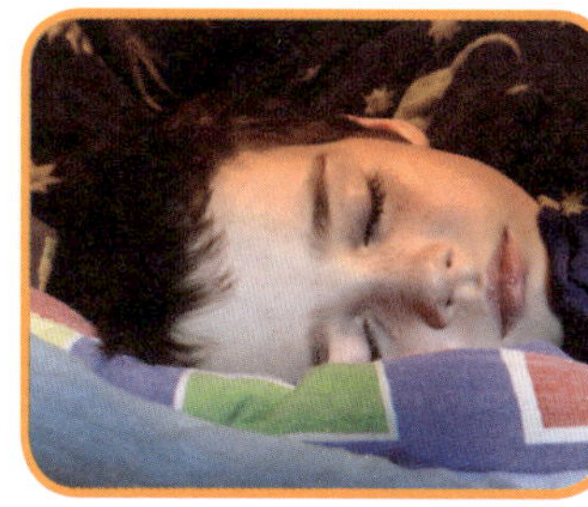

I drink lots of water/ juice.

I eat a lot of sweets/ fruit.

I watch TV/ play with my friends.

I go to bed every night /day.

9 Draw a picture of the correct behaviour.

Sit correctly. →

Walk in the classroom. →

Cover your mouth when you cough. →

Let's investigate at home!

Make a healthy habits chart

1

Design and colour a healthy habits chart.

2

Put it in the kitchen.

3

Practise the healthy habits every day.

4

Put a sticker on your chart when you complete each goal.

1 Write.

What is your favourite fruit? ____________

What is your favourite sport? ____________

Skills check

1 Look at the pictures. Look at the letters. Write the words.

a p p l e

aplpe
apple

1

_ _ _ _ _

bread
brade

2

_ _ _ _

egsg
eggs

3

_ _ _ _

milk
mikl

4

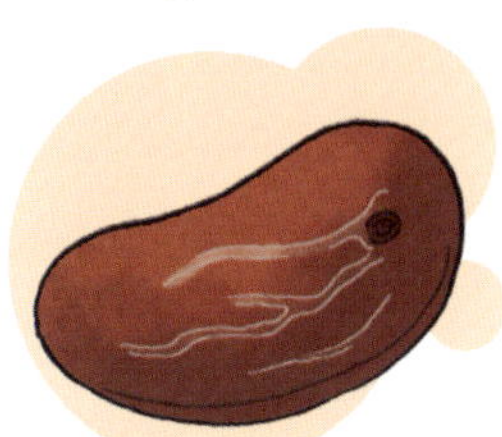

_ _ _ _

meta
meat

5

_ _ _ _

nuts
nust

UNIT 3 Living things

1 Write.

grow reproduce die ~~born~~

Living things are born.

Living things ______.

Living things ______.

Living things ______.

2 Circle the living things.

treeduckpuppysnailsquirrelgrasskitten

3 Write.

~~flowers~~ seeds roots leaves

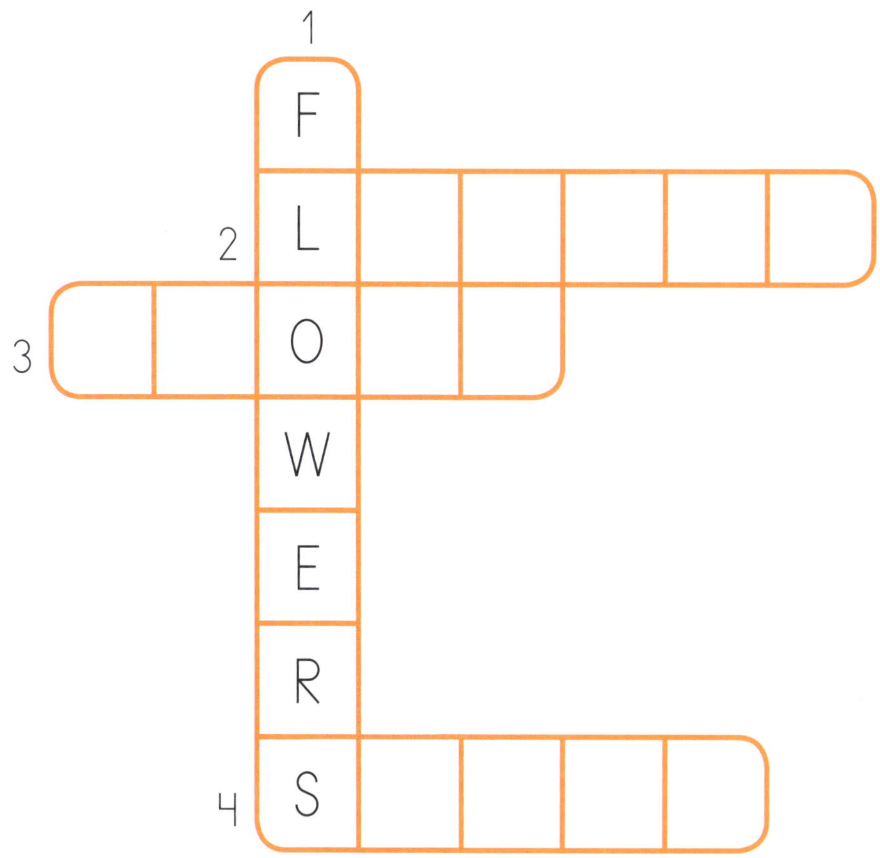

4 What do plants need? Circle.

air

ball

water

sunlight

house

5 Match.

piglet | puppy | kitten | chick

6 Complete the table. Write *yes* or *no*.

	they are born	they grow	they reproduce	they die
 plants	yes			
 toys				
 animals				
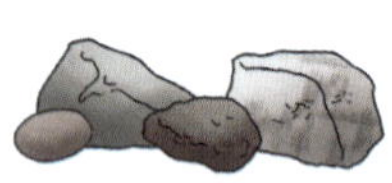 rocks				

7 Complete the sentence with words from the table.

__________ and __________ are living things.

8 Colour the non-living things in the picture.

9 Write.

bird

kite

bag

boy

tree

bin

living things	non-living things
bird	

Let's investigate at home!

Make a mini photo album

1

Cut out your album.

2

Fold on the lines.

3

Glue photos of you at different ages. Write your age.

4

Decorate the cover of your album.

1 Write.

How old are you? ______________________

How tall are you? ______________________

Skills check

1 Look and read. Write *yes* or *no*.

Example: There is a man with a dog. yes

1. The people are at the beach. ______
2. Two people are sitting on a bench. ______
3. A bird is a living thing. ______
4. A kite is a living thing. ______

1 Circle the invertebrates.

2 Look and write.

vertebrates				
mammal	bird	reptile	amphibian	fish
				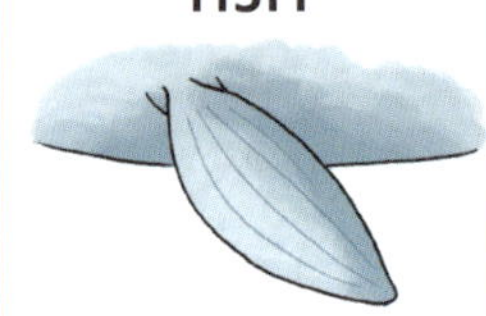
monkey				

shark

snake

monkey

frog

duck

3 Write.

walk fly ~~swim~~ slither

Fish swim.

Cows ______.

Snakes ______.

Bats ______.

4 Match.

oviparous animals

viviparous animals

5 Write.

parrot

sheep

shark

herbivore	carnivore	omnivore

6 Do they live on land or in water? Write.

dolphin fish ant octopus chicken mouse

7 Colour.

wild domestic

8 Read and write the correct animal.

canary

zebra

snake

penguin

I'm black and white.
I have wings but I can't fly. I can swim.
I'm a ______.

I'm oviparous.
I'm yellow.
I slither.
I'm a ______.

Let's investigate at home!

Make a chicken life cycle wheel

1

Cut out two circles.

2

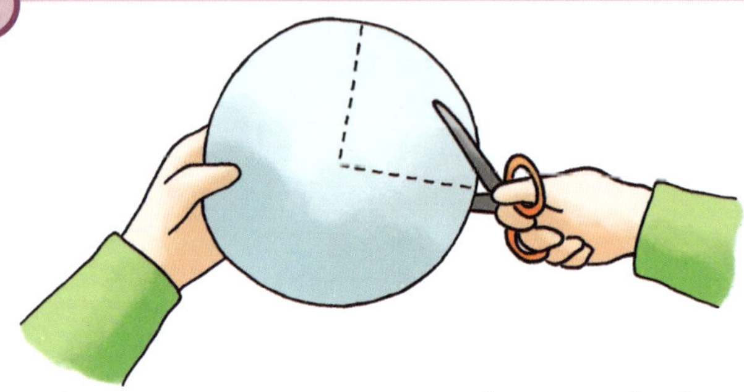

Cut out a quarter of one circle.

3

Draw and colour the four stages of a chicken's life on the other circle.

4

Fasten the two circles together.

1 Write the correct word.

chick oviparous eggs

Chickens lay ______. A baby chicken is called a ______. Birds are ______.

Skills check

1 Look at the pictures. Look at the letters. Write the words.

m o n k e y

e k o y m n

1

....

e o r h s

2

....

s e n a k

3

....

c d k u

4

....

i e s d p r

5

....

g r e t i

UNIT 5 What is it made of?

1 Write.

wood glass fabric ~~plastic~~ metal paper

plastic

2 Write.

cotton

plastic

natural

cotton

manufactured

glass

wood

3 Write the properties of these objects.

Is it hard or soft?	 hard		
Is it smooth or rough?			
Is it bendy or rigid?			
Is it shiny or dull?			

4 Colour.

transparent   opaque

5 Do the materials change shape? Write *yes* or *no*.

	bend 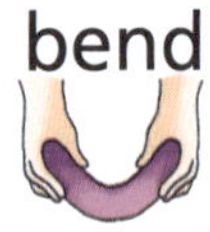	stretch 	squeeze 
	yes	no	yes

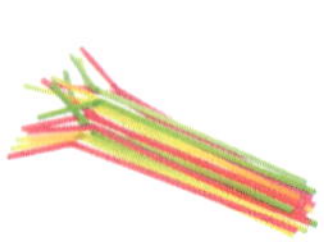			

6 Trace the lines with blue (cold) or red (heat).

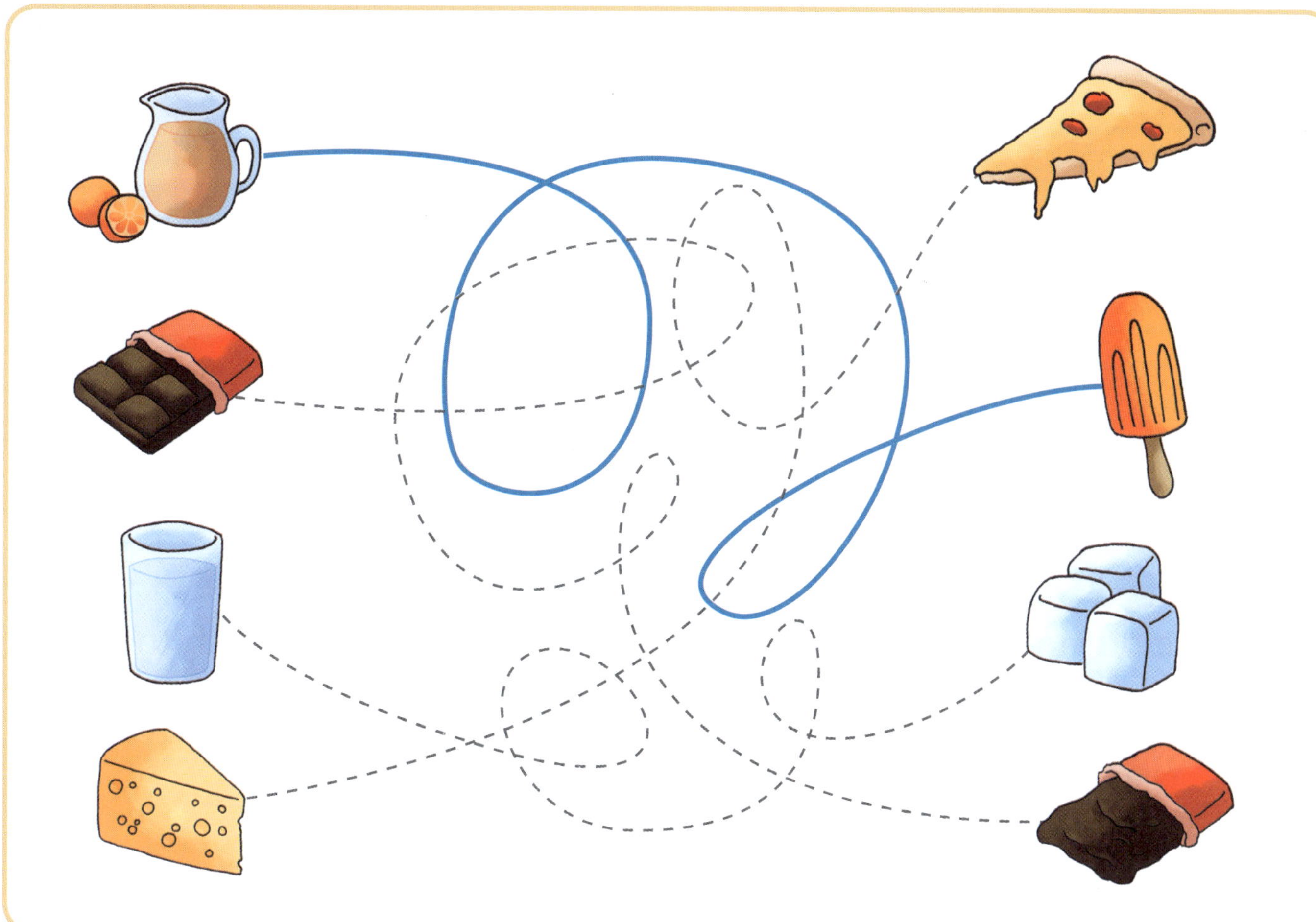

7 Draw your favourite toy. Write.

my favourite toy

Is it hard or soft?

It's ______________.

Is it shiny or dull?

It's ______________.

Is it transparent or opaque?

It's ______________.

Let's investigate at home!

Find different materials at home

1

Write different properties of materials.

2

Look for an object with those properties.

3

Draw and colour a picture of the object.

4

Write the material it is made of.

1 Write.

Which object can you bend? __________

Which object can you stretch? __________

Which object can you squeeze? __________

Skills check

1 **Look and read. Put a tick or a cross. Look at the two examples.**

It's hard. ✓

It's transparent. ✗

1 It's a natural material. ☐

2 It's made of cotton. ☐

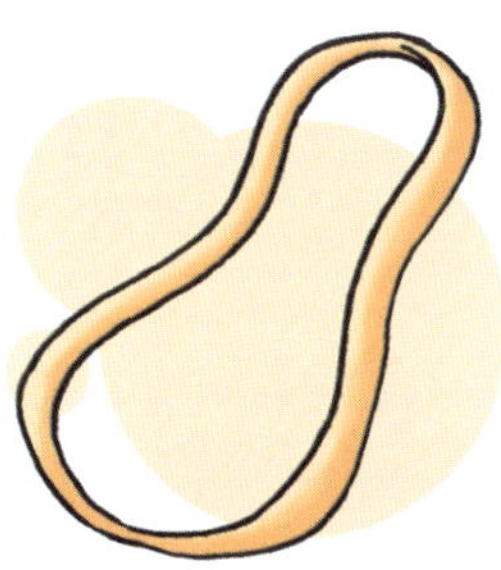

3 It's rigid. ☐

4 It's smooth. ☐

5 It's shiny. ☐

UNIT 6 How does it work?

1 Write the machines you use at school.

computer

screwdriver

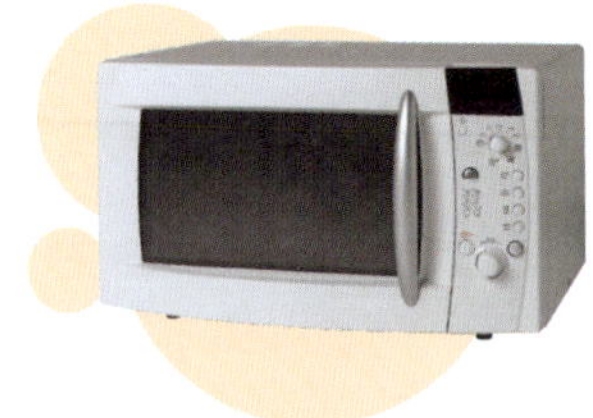

microwave

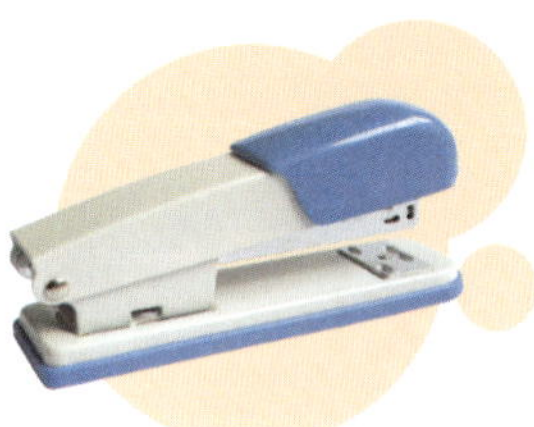

stapler

stapler

sharpener

hammer

scissors

2 Colour the complex machines.

3 Circle and write.

radio trumpet

A radio needs electricity.

TV book

A ______ needs electricity.

lamp bicycle

A ______ needs electricity.

fridge bottle

A ______ needs electricity.

4 Match. Write *a few* or *lots of*.

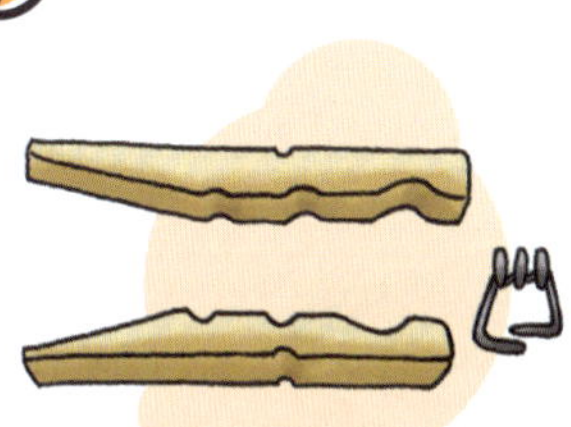

It has ______ parts.

It has ______ parts.

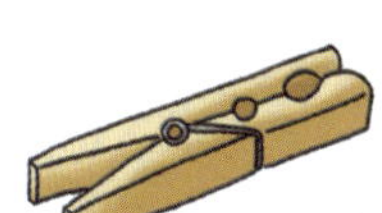

It has a few parts.

5 Write.

spade hammer spoon ~~scissors~~

A hairdresser uses scissors.

A chef uses a ______.

A gardener uses a ______.

A builder uses a ______.

6 Look and draw what is missing.

- [x] keyboard
- [x] disk drive
- [x] printer
- [ ] screen
- [ ] mouse

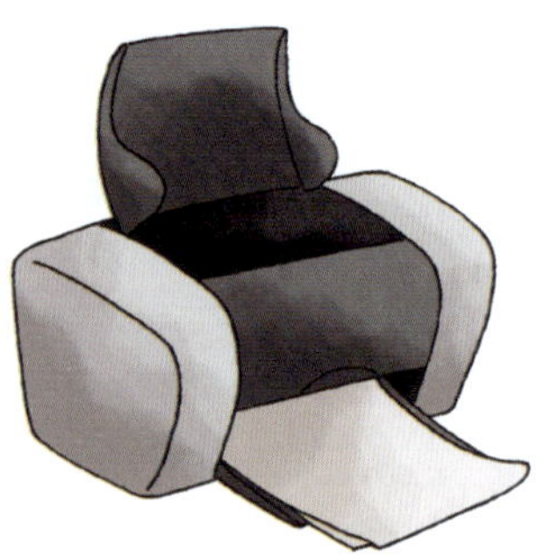

7 Write.

watch

toaster

lamp

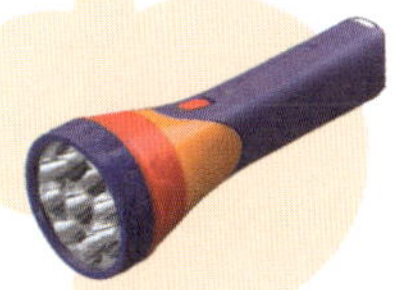
torch

camera

TV

batteries

mains

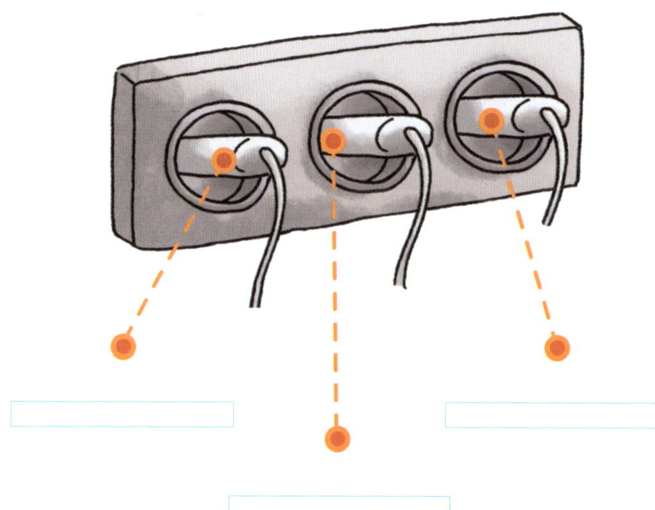

8 Circle the dangerous behaviour.

Let's investigate at home!

Make a paper helicopter

1

Draw a design.

2

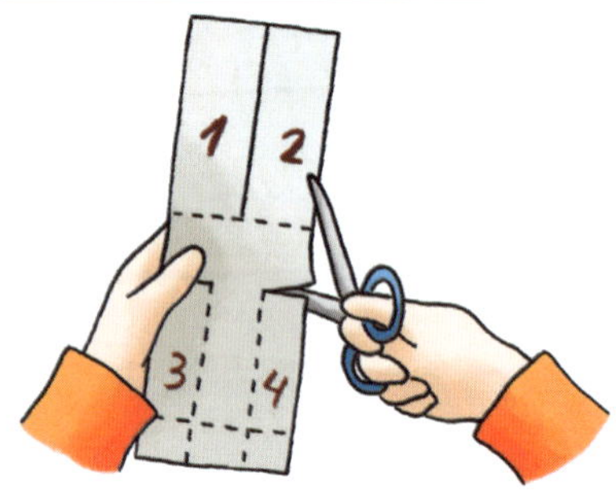

Cut along the lines.

3

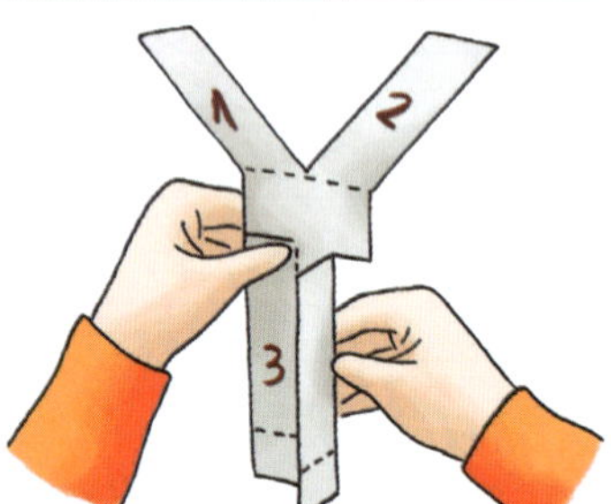

Fold along the dotted lines.

4

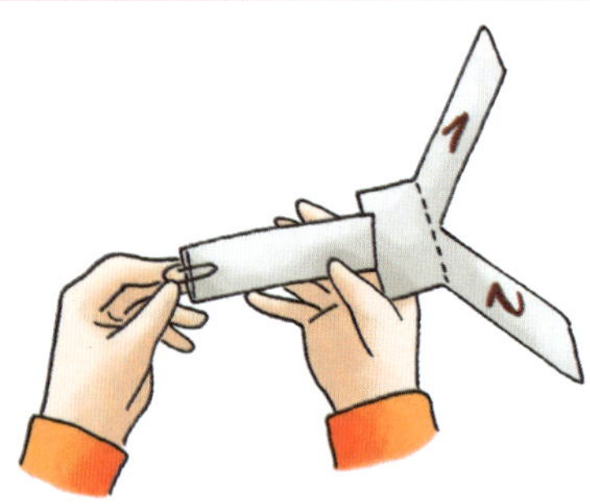

Attach a paper clip.

1 Write *yes* or *no*.

Does your helicopter spin? ______

Does your helicopter need electricity? ______

Skills check

1 **Look and read. Write *yes* or *no*.**

Example: A car is a simple machine. no

1. The man is taking a photo. ______
2. There are two wheels in the picture. ______
3. A bicycle has lots of parts. ______
4. A bicycle needs electricity. ______
5. A watch uses batteries. ______

Glossary

English	Your language

UNIT 1: All about me

happy	
sad	
angry	
worried	
see	
hear	
smell	
taste	
touch	

UNIT 2: Healthy habits

breakfast	
lunch	
dinner	
healthy snack	
a cold	
tummy ache	
headache	

English	Your language

UNIT 3: Living things

be born	
grow	
reproduce	
die	
seeds	
roots	
leaves	
flowers	

UNIT 4: Animals

vertebrate	
invertebrate	
skeleton	
walk	
fly	
swim	
slither	

Glossary

English	Your language

UNIT 5: What is it made of?

metal	
paper	
fabric	
wood	
glass	
plastic	
bend	
stretch	
squeeze	

UNIT 6: How does it work?

scissors	
mop	
pulley	
car	
microwave	
computer	
mains	
batteries	